CRAFT BOX

Craft Like

THE ANCIENT GREEKS

Jillian Powell

PowerKiDS press

Published in 2018 by **The Rosen Publishing Group, Inc.**
29 East 21st Street, New York, NY 10010

Cataloging-in-Publication Data
Names: Powell, Jillian.
Title: Craft like the ancient Greeks / Jillian Powell.
Description: New York : Powerkids Press, 2018. | Series: Craft box | Includes index.
Identifiers: ISBN 9781508155980 (pbk.) | ISBN 9781499433661 (library bound) | ISBN 9781499433586 (6 pack)
Subjects: LCSH: Greece--Civilization--To 146 B.C.--Juvenile literature. | Handicraft--Juvenile literature.
Classification: LCC DF77.P68 2018 | DDC 938--dc23

Editor: Elizabeth Brent
Designer: Rocket Design (East Anglia) Ltd
Craft stylist: Annalees Lim
Photographer: Simon Pask, N1 Studios

Picture acknowledgments: All step-by-step craft photography: Simon Pask,
N1 Studios; images used throughout for creative graphics: Shutterstock.

Manufactured in China
CPSIA Compliance Information: Batch #BS17PK: For Further Information contact
Rosen Publishing, New York, New York at 1-800-237-9932

A NOTE ABOUT MEASUREMENTS

Measurements are given in U.S. form with metric in parentheses. The metric conversion is rounded to make it easier to measure.

Contents

the Ancient Greeks

The ancient Greeks lived from about 3000–430 BCE.

The ancient Greeks lived more than 3,000 years ago on the mainland and islands of Greece and in **colonies** in Europe and North Africa. A farming and seafaring people, they lived in independent city-states, trading amongst themselves and the colonies.

Ancient Greek writers and **philosophers**, such as Plato and Aristotle, developed ideas that still shape the way we think and do things today.

The ancient Greeks enjoyed the arts. They built huge stone theaters for performing and watching plays. **Sculptors** carved statues and decorated temples such as the Parthenon, built to worship the many gods and goddesses of Greek religion and **mythology**.

Ancient Greek craftsmen were skilled at working with materials including **marble**, clay, metals, wood, and leather. They were mostly "free men" who used slaves as assistants. Some came from the colonies, bringing new skills. Their workshops were grouped together in cities, so areas became known for one craft, such as **pottery** or leather tanning.

Greek buildings and objects, from temples and **sculptures** to pottery and jewelry, can tell us lots of fascinating facts about life in ancient Greece. They can also inspire you to make some Greek crafts of your own!

make
Theater masks

The ancient Greeks went to the theater to watch plays by great playwrights such as Sophocles. Actors wore masks made from wood, linen, or leather to show different characters and emotions in comedies or tragic dramas.

You will need:

- Large foil plates
- Scissors
- Marker
- Sticky tape
- Craft sticks
- Metallic paint
- Brush
- Foil or foil chocolate wrappers
- Glue
- Glitter glue

1 Cut away two foil plates to make two mask shapes.

2 Hold each mask up to your face and mark where to place the eyes and mouth. Draw them on, then use the scissors to make holes and cut around the lines. Cover the cut edges with sticky tape.

3 Paint the craft sticks with metallic paint.

4 Cut thin strips of foil or foil chocolate wrappers and attach them to the mask to make hair or beards.

5 Glue or tape a craft stick onto the back of each mask.

6 Cut thin strips of foil and glue them to the face of each mask to make frown lines. Use glitter glue to draw a nose onto each mask, and to go around the mouth and eyes, exaggerating the happy or sad expression.

Did you know ...
Women weren't allowed to act, so men wore masks and played the female roles.

make a
Fish dish

Potters made pots, bowls, and dishes of all shapes and sizes for storing and serving food and drinks in ancient Greece. They used red and black clay and decorated it with animals, birds, or characters from myths.

You will need:
- Plain and **terracotta** air-dry clay
- Rolling pin
- Clay tools
- Black paint
- Brush

1 Take a piece of plain clay and work it with your hands to soften it. Roll it flat then use a clay tool to cut a circle to make a base for the dish.

2 Take a larger piece of plain clay and mold it with your hands to form a shallow dish shape. Shape a dip in the middle of the dish.

3 Attach the dish to the base. Then roll two pieces of plain clay to form the handles and attach one to each side of the dish.

4 Roll a piece of terracotta clay flat. Use the craft knife to cut out three fish shapes. Cut out eye holes and make small slits along their bodies.

Did you know ...
The dip in the middle of fish dishes was for fish sauce or oil.

5 Press the terracotta clay shapes onto the plain clay dish while it is still soft. Allow the clay to air dry.

6 Paint the whole dish black apart from the terracotta fish.

make a
Medusa headdress

Medusa is one of the most famous characters in Greek mythology. The goddess Athena cursed Medusa, making snakes grow out of her head instead of hair. Medusa could turn anyone who looked directly at her into stone.

1

Paint the hair band and the Styrofoam eggs with green acrylic paint and allow to dry. Placing the band and eggs on toothpicks stuck into Styrofoam will make this easier.

2

Glue two red sequins or fake gems onto each Styrofoam egg to look like snakes' eyes.

3

Take a pair of pipe cleaners and twist them together. Repeat until you have several snake bodies.

4 Use the scissors to expose the wires at one end of the pipe cleaners and push each one firmly into a Styrofoam egg.

5 Twist the other end of the snake around the hair band. Repeat with the remaining snakes, working around the band.

6 Wind more pipe cleaners around the band to hide the snake pipe cleaner ends. Fold down the sharp ends to make sure they don't hurt you. Then bend the snakes' bodies into slithery shapes.

Did you know ...
Women in ancient Greece wore head bands made from metal or ribbons.

11

make an Olympic torch

The Olympic Games began in ancient Greece over 2,700 years ago. They were held in honor of the god **Zeus**. A torch was lit every four years at the start of the Olympics and burned throughout the Games.

1 Cut out a piece of card stock in the shape of a triangle.

2 Cut out and glue on wrapping paper to cover the triangle.

3 Cut a piece of gold mesh fabric and tape it onto the wrapping paper.

4 Roll the triangle into a cone and glue or tape the edges together.

Did you know ... Greek Olympic champions were awarded olive wreaths which they wore like crowns.

5 Snip jagged edges into several pieces of red and yellow cellophane, then scrunch them up to form flames.

6 Bunch the cellophane together then glue it around the inside edges of the cone.

make a
Perfume bottle

An aryballos was a small flask used in ancient Greece to hold perfumes or bathing oils. It could be shaped like a globe, a shell, an animal, a face, or even a foot! Some aryballoi had cords for wearing around the wrist or hanging from wall pegs.

You will need:

- Balloon
- Card stock
- Masking tape
- Scissors
- Cardboard
- White glue and water
- Tissue paper
- Paper towel
- Acrylic paints
- Brushes
- Black cord/ribbon

1 Blow up a small round balloon. Tape a thin strip of card stock, about ¾ inch (2 cm) wide, into a circle to make a base for the bottle.

2 Make a strip of card stock 1 inch by 5 inches (2.5 cm by 13 cm) and tape it into a circle. Tape it to the top of the balloon to make the bottle neck.

3 Cut a circle of cardboard the same diameter as the bottle neck to close the lower end. Tape it to the bottle neck.

4 To make paper-mâché, mix equal amounts of white glue and water. Dip strips of tissue paper into the glue mix, then smooth them onto the sides of the balloon and card stock. Finish with a layer of paper towel and allow the bottle to dry.

Did you know ...
Ancient Greek bathers used a "strigil," or metal scraper, to clean themselves.

5 Paint the bottle and allow it to dry, then decorate it. Look at pictures of Greek aryballoi in books and on the internet to give you ideas.

6 Cut a piece of cord or ribbon and tie it around the bottle neck.

make a
Golden wreath

The ancient Greeks wore wreaths made from **grape vines** for the festival of the wine god Dionysus. Wreaths made from gold were worn for religious ceremonies, left as gifts for the gods at temples, and placed in burial **tombs**.

You will need:

- ◎ Large paper plate
- ◎ Scissors
- ◎ Gold wrapping paper, foil, or card stock
- ◎ Glue
- ◎ Gold candy wrappers
- ◎ Fine gold craft wire
- ◎ Gold glitter glue

1 Cut the rim off the paper plate to make a base for your wreath. Then cut out a short section and snip the ends into points.

2 Cut out vine leaves of different sizes from gold foil, card stock, or wrapping paper.

3 Fold the leaves in half, and open them out again.

4

Glue the leaves onto the rim base, facing in different directions. The leaves on the right side of the wreath should point towards the right end, the leaves on the left should point to the left end.

Did you know ...
The Greeks wore wreaths made from myrtle leaves for weddings and feasts.

5

Scrunch small pieces of gold foil or candy wrappers into balls. Cut short lengths of craft wire and wind each piece around two or three gold balls, leaving a long end free.

6

Wind the end of each piece of wire around the wreath base and glue on more leaves to hide the wire. Decorate your wreath with glitter glue.

make a
Fibula

In ancient Greece, men and women wore simple tunics called chitons made from linen. The tunics were pinned at the shoulders with a pin called a fibula.

1

Paint the popsicle stick with the metallic gold paint or paint pen and allow it to dry.

2

Wind the craft wire around a piece of gold cord and then roll the cord into a spiral. Repeat, so you have two cord spirals.

3

Cut out pieces of card stock and glue the cord spirals to them. Then cut around the spirals.

4 Glue the spirals card stock-side down to each end of the stick.

Did you know …
Gold, silver, **bronze**, amber and bone were used to make fibulae.

5 Decorate the middle of the stick by winding more gold cord around it.

6 Tape the safety pin to the other side of the popsicle stick, so you can pin it on.

make a
Hoplite's shield

Greek foot soldiers were called hoplites because their large shields were called hoplons. Hoplons were made from wood, covered with bronze or leather, and decorated with symbols or characters from Greek mythology.

1 Cut out a circle of black card stock larger than the paper plate.

2 Fold the red paper in half and cut a line of triangles along the fold, then cut along the fold. Repeat to make enough triangles to go around the edge of the circle and then glue them to the card stock.

3 Cover the plate with gold foil and glue it rim-side down onto the middle of the card stock.

4 Cut four narrow strips of red paper and glue them onto the front of the shield to make the Greek letter lambda. It looks like an upside-down V.

Did you know ...
The lambda became a symbol that represented Sparta. Before the lambda, hoplites had unique symbols on their shields.

5 Paint on dots of glitter glue around the lambda and the rim of your shield.

6 Cut a wide strip of card stock, fold it back at each end and glue or tape it onto the back of the shield to form a handle.

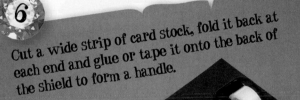

make a
Greek arm guard

Greek soldiers wore arm guards made of bronze in battle. The guards covered and protected their arms from the wrist to the elbow.

1

Draw a shape like the one in the picture onto a piece of card stock, and cut it out. It should be big enough to cover your forearm.

2

Bend the card stock to form a tube that will fit around your arm and tape the edges together.

3

For papier-mâché, mix up equal amounts of water and white glue. Tear thin strips of tissue paper and smooth them onto the card stock. Continue laying on more strips of paper, making criss-cross patterns, and allow them to dry.

4 Cut some pieces of string and glue them around both edges of the tube. Glue two long pieces onto the tube to make a curved symmetrical pattern.

Did you know ...
Hoplites also wore helmets, breast plates, and leg guards made from bronze.

5 Look for the point where the card stock template was taped together and cut the tube open along this line so you can fit it around your arm.

6 Paint the arm guard using gold metallic paint and leave it to dry. Decorate with paper fasteners, making sure you tape the ends down inside the arm guard.

make a

Gable decoration

The Greeks decorated the roofs and **gables** of buildings and grand tombs with **carved sculptures called acroteria**. They were made from stone, marble, or painted terracotta.

1

Roll out and trim a piece of clay to make a rectangular base 5 inches by 2 inches (12 cm by 5 cm) and 1/2 inch (1 cm) thick.

2

Roll out and cut two strips of clay 11 inches by 3 inches (28 cm by 8 cm) wide.

3

Curl the strips into scrolls, then press them down onto the base facing opposite ways.

4

Shape a piece of clay into a diamond and use a tool to make a groove around it. Press it down between the scrolls and fill any gaps with clay.

Did you know ...
Carved statues were also used as acroteria.

5

Roll out and cut seven strips of clay 4 inches by 2 inches (10 cm by 5 cm) wide.

6

Make seven small balls of clay and place one in the center of each strip. Fold each strip in half, and press onto the scrolls. Allow to dry.

make a
Discus

Discus throwing was a popular sport at the ancient Greek Olympics. Athletes competed to see who could throw a heavy discus made from iron or bronze over the longest distance.

1 Glue the paper plates together rim to rim.

2 Paint the plates using gray-brown or metallic paint to look like bronze.

3 Use the compass to draw three concentric circles on the back of each plate. Go over the circles with marker.

4

Use glitter glue to go over each circle.

Did you know ...
The word "alphabet" comes from the ancient Greek letters for A and B.

5

Use the metallic or white pen to decorate the discus. You could write letters from the Greek alphabet. You can find the full alphabet on the internet!

make
Pan pipes

Pan pipes are named after the Greek god Pan. Greek mythology says that he made pipes from water **reeds** to play music for his lost love, Syrinx. Still played in many parts of the world, pan pipes can be made from reeds, **bamboo**, wood, and other materials.

1

To make different notes, each pipe will be a different length. The lengths should increase gradually as shown here.

2

Take a small piece of clay and flatten it. Press one end of each straw into it, then pull it out to plug the end of the straw. Cover the ends of each straw with tape, to stop the clay from falling out.

3

Cover one side of a craft stick with double-sided tape. Repeat for the other stick.

4

Stick the straws to the craft stick, starting with the longest and finishing with the shortest. Leave small, equal gaps between them. The open tops should be in a line just above the stick.

Did you know …

Pan pipes are one of the oldest musical instruments, dating back 6,000 years.

5

Press the other stick, taped-side down, on top, then paint both sides and allow to dry. Once the pipes are dry, remove the clay.

6

Tie a piece of twine around the sticks to carry or hang the pan pipes. Play notes by blowing across the top of each straw.

Glossary

Bamboo A tall plant with a hollow, woody stem.

Bronze An orange-brown metal made from a mix of copper and tin.

Colony A country under the political rule of another country.

Compass: A tool with two arms, one sharp and one with a pencil, that can be used to draw circles or arcs.

Discus A heavy disc thrown in athletics competitions.

Gable The triangular part of a wall between two roofs.

Grape vine The plant, or vine, on which grapes grow.

Linen A fabric made from a plant called flax.

Marble A hard stone that can be polished.

Mythology A collection of ancient stories about gods, heroes, and magical beasts.

Philosopher A great thinker.

Potter A person who makes pottery.

Pottery Pots, dishes, and other objects made from baked clay.

Reed A plant with a long, thin stem that grows near water.

Sculptor A person who makes sculptures.

Sculpture A work of art that has been carved, modeled, or cast in materials such as stone, wood, and bronze.

Seafaring Traveling by sea.

Shield A piece of armor carried by soldiers to protect themselves against weapon strikes.

Terracotta Brownish-red pottery or clay.

Tomb A small building that acts as a grave, where someone's body is put when they die.

Zeus Greek god of the sky, and ruler of all the Olympian gods.

Further information

BOOKS

Ancient Greece
Anne Pearson
DK Children, 2014

Greek Mythology (Ken Jennings' Junior Genius Guides)
Ken Jennings
Little Simon, 2014

Top Ten Worst Things About Ancient Greece
Victoria England
Gareth Stevens, 2012

WEBSITES

PowerKids Press has developed an online list of websites related to the subject of this book. This site is updated regularly. Please use this link to access the list:

www.powerkidslinks.com/cb/greeks

Index